Are you a Spiritual Hypochondriac?

By

Dottie Randazzo

Are you a Spiritual Hypochondriac?

by

Dottie Randazzo

Published by:

Creative Dreaming

6433 Topanga Cyn. Blvd.

Woodland Hills, CA 91303

ISBN 978-0-6151-8006-9

By Dottie Randazzo

Praying 101 for Spiritual Enlightenment

Praying 101 for Men

Praying 101 for Women

Praying 101 for Kids & Teens

Praying 101 for Parents

The Feeling

Trust

It's OK to be human.

If you are constantly running from one book to another, one movie to another, one spiritual guru to another and/or one organization to another, could it possibly be that you are a Spiritual Hypochondriac?

A hypochondriac is someone who worries or talks excessively about their health.

A Spiritual
Hypochondriac is
someone who worries
or talks excessively
about his or her
spirituality.

Are you worried that you need to be fixed spiritually? Do you run from book to book, guru to guru, class to class thinking that the next book, the next class or the next guru will fix you?

Before we go on, I want to make it clear, I am not advocating books, gurus or classes should be avoided.

It's like the writer who takes every class and reads every book on writing, but never puts a pen to the pad to write, always thinking that something else must be learned first.

Or, what about the individual who reads every book or article on eating healthy, yet has not even eaten a walnut or blueberry?

Or, what about the artist who takes class after class, reading every book, and the only art he or she has ever produced are class assignments?

Some spiritual teachings require an enormous amount of time.

I will not name names, but at one point in my life, I was spending 40 to 60 hours a week to obtain "The Light of My Creator." This was in addition to working full time and sleeping.

I asked repeatedly, "How can I use my God-given creative abilities to create a great life if I am always here trying to get more Light, which will enable me to create a great life?"

I was exhausted. I personally didn't want any more Light. I felt I had earned enough Light and now wanted to cash in and put it to work creating my great life.

I left the organization
and, as you can
imagine, I wasn't
patted on the back and
wished well as I
walked out the door.

Instead, I was informed that by leaving I would not get any more Light, which was personally fine with me. Remember, I had a ton of Light in the bank, from 15 months of 40 to 60 hours a week of getting Light.

I was on my way to creating a remarkable life.

I occasionally get calls from this organization to see if I have run out of Light. I tell them that I am doing great, and am glad that I got to experience them. I remind them, as they taught me, "There is an abundance of Light available to all."

Glad to know there isn't a Light shortage.

I was told if I want or need more Light to call them. Light pushers, they are, just like every paid commercial on TV, trying to give or sell me something in which I already had enough.

I want to make you
aware of the state of
your spiritual health.

Do you beat yourself up when something negative happens to you, believing that you have failed in your spiritual evolution, or that you have just taken 10 steps back in your spiritual evolution?

I used to. And very often, someone would remind me, "Hello, you are human."

And I would respond, "Yeah, but I thought I was spiritually evolved and now this or that has happened. This or that happens to other people who aren't as spiritually evolved as I."

Hummm… was that my ego talking or what?

I began to feel a lot better about my spiritual evolution when I realized no matter how much I evolved, things, circumstances and situations will continue to happen.

I have evolved enough to know that it is more important how we handle situations than how we let situations affect us.

No matter how
evolved I get, a broken
heart will still hurt.
Finding out I have
been lied to will still
be disappointing.

I would not change these feelings for anything in the world. After all, I can't even begin to imagine what a non-feeling life would be like.

Because I have experienced a broken heart, I can feel compassion towards someone who has a broken heart.

Because I have experienced disappointment in another, I can be compassionate and comforting to the individual who is feeling disappointment.

It's OK to be human.

I am sure you have heard the analogy that life is like an onion. You peel away one layer only to discover another one and yet another one.

Yep, like life you fix one thing and then before you know it, there is another thing to be fixed and you work hard to fix it.

By God, you will spiritually evolve and then, when you think you got it all finally taken care of and everything is going smoothly, out of nowhere comes an issue confronting you with an uncomfortable feeling that you thought should not be happening to you.

For God's sake, you are spiritually evolved. You put in the time, you read the books, and you had the guru.

I know the feeling.
You are tired. When
will it all be finished?

When will you finally get it right?

You feel sad. You feel as if you have failed. You feel as if you have been working your way to the head of the line and now you have been informed you must go to the back of the line.

How could this be?

Life isn't fair.

This isn't right.

You are tired and depressed. You wonder when you will be able to find the strength to pick yourself up, dust yourself off, and continue with your spiritual evolution.

You may even have done what I have done in the past.

I walked into a hypnotist's office and said "I'm tired of fixing myself only to discover something else needs to be dealt with. Can you just hypnotize me and fix it all, even the stuff I am not even aware of that needs to be fixed? If there is a chance that I could start cursing profusely after the age of 55, can we

just hypnotize me so
that when, or if, I get
to that bridge, I will be
spiritually evolved so
I won't have to deal
with it?"

My thinking was, much like bug extermination, instead of a spray for ants and a spray for flies and a spray for another bug, let's just use a blanket bomb! Let's deal with it in one shot.

The hypnotist was shocked and I began to wonder, "Surely, I am not the first person to say fix me, even fix what we aren't aware of that's broken."

She asked me why I wanted to be fixed, which baffled me. Don't we all want to be 100% fixed?

She reminded me that life was school, and when I am fixed in this lifetime, I will be ready for the next lifetime with its challenges that I will want to fix.

Well, I am here to tell you that I am not ready to be finished with this lifetime.

So I came to terms
with the fact that I was
not finished living
this life, so I would
not rush to fix what I
am not even aware of
that needs to be fixed.

Hey, I was just looking to be spiritually efficient.

I discovered no value
in being spiritually
efficient, however.

In facts, worrying about spiritual issues before they arise clearly is the sign of a Spiritual Hypochondriac.

Why would someone want to be spiritually fixed?

There are only two reasons I have come up with so far: 1) to avoid life's ups and downs, and 2) to get a passing grade at the end. Neither of these reasons is valid.

After all, life is like a
roller coaster.

So saying you want a life without ups and downs is like saying you'll only ride a roller coaster that goes in a straight line - no hills and drops, no flips, no turns, just straight.

Would life really be worth living if it didn't have high points or low points?

If it didn't have any high points and low points and all the points were the same, you wouldn't be feeling good or bad, happy or sad, excited or disappointed. You actually wouldn't feel a thing.

Doesn't sound very interesting, does it?

Let's explore the second reason you might want to pursue spiritual efficiency.

What's it going to be like for you when you leave this world?

Will you leave this earth on a cloud, in a puff of smoke, a ball of light, or will you be as you are in physical form standing at the pearly white gates holding your Bible and/or beads?

You *will* have your Bible and/or beads with you, right?

Will you be poised for
the examination of
your life?

Will you proudly recite the prayers and/or Bible verses you have spent a lifetime memorizing?

Will you show up with your attendance record of the classes you took and/or services you have attended?

If you think living your life is equivalent to preparing for a spelling bee, you just might be on the right track.

But what if it isn't going to be like that?

What if you show up
to the place that you
believe you will show
up to and you find out
none of what you
thought would make a
difference actually
does?

What if memorizing, quoting, and/or attendance do not mean a thing?

Whatcha gonna do?

Imagine that you have arrived at the pearly white gates and you can't speak. You have no voice. You open your mouth, but nothing comes out.

In front of you, the movie of your life will be played with no sound.

You will be judged on
your actions only.

You will not be judged on the books you read, the classes you took, the gurus you rubbed elbows with, your attendance record, or what you have spent a lifetime memorizing.

Would you be allowed in?

I am sure this question cannot be answered quickly. After all, you would have to replay the movie of your life without all the talking.

This may be hard to imagine, but if you really wanted to, you could reevaluate the life you have lived based on your actions only.

This would be the
fairest judgment of all.

After all, words are merely words and action speaks volumes!

We have determined you are human, and if you are anxious about being fixed spiritually, you may be a Spiritual Hypochondriac.

So what about when
bad things happen to
spiritually good
people? Are they
being punished by the
Gods? Have they
failed in their spiritual
evolution?

Actually, it is the opposite.

While a situation may appear bad and feel just awful, it is often propelling you to a better place.

Some consider this a quantum leap, and quantum leaps don't feel very good.

An example of a quantum leap for the better would be your computer getting the blue screen of death. During this bad situation, you may discover it is time to upgrade your computer. You may discover information regarding your back-up system that you would not have been aware of otherwise.

You may upgrade your software. You may discover your computer guy is no longer working on computers. You may be introduced to a more qualified computer guy. Look at the discoveries or challenges this seemingly dooming situation offers. You will, in the end, be in a better place than you

were the day before
you got the dreaded
blue screen of death.

Sometimes you must
go down a bad road to
get to a better place.

In the end, you will
have a more efficient
computer, updated
software, knowledge
about your back-up
system (was it

working or not?), and you may or may not have a new computer guy.

You do everything possible to prevent disasters from happening. However, often times, disasters are necessary to get you to a better place faster than if the disaster had not occurred.

Think about it. If you hadn't gotten the blue screen of death on your computer, when would you have upgraded it? When would you have upgraded your programs? When would you have checked to see if your back-up system was, indeed, still backing up? When would you have found out your computer guy was no longer working on computers?

You have a job you really dislike. You know you should be doing something else. You dislike the commute, the people you work with, the work you do and your salary. Yet, you are shocked when you are handed your pink slip and fired. Your next job is more conveniently located to where you live; you enjoy the people, the work and the pay. Was getting fired really a bad thing? Were you really going to find the courage to leave the job you loathed? Probably not, so the Master(s) of the Universe, or God, helped you along, pushing you out of the nest like the mama bird does to her baby bird. It's all about getting you in a better place, even if it doesn't feel good.

You have been dumped. It hurts and your heart feels broken. You weren't 100% happy in the relationship. You didn't like the emotional roller coaster and unpredictability of your partner. You felt uncomfortable with his or her alcohol consumption. You and his or her views of what a relationship should be were totally different. Yet, you felt betrayed, shocked and hurt that he or she chose to end the relationship. You are human. Was it really a bad thing that this person ended the relationship? Were they really doing you a favor without realizing it? You are now in a position to pursue relationships that are more comfortable to you. Did you have to get dumped for the relationship to end? Chances are, you probably would not have had the courage to end the relationship. This is an example of the bad road one must travel to get in a better place.

Let's talk about Hurricane Katrina. I can talk firsthand about this subject, since 99% of my family was affected by it. It was very devastating to those directly involved and those who knew someone. I think that what is acutely obvious is the value that was placed material things. Tears were cried over glass vases that were once owned by a relative that passed away 20 years before Katrina. More tears were cried over sentimental belongings. Some were forced to begin lives in other parts of the country, parts of the country they would never have experienced otherwise. Some got jobs they never would have had if Katrina had not come along. Some met people they would have never met otherwise. Some people moved to better homes. Some got their homes that needed a lot of work before Katrina rebuilt. Some learned how fragile their relationships were when put through the test of a devastating event. Some learned firsthand what the kindness of strangers was like. Yes, it was a very bad road that most had to travel down to get in a better place.

So are bad things really bad? When they look and feel like bad things, are they really bad? Or, is it us taking quantum leaps in our spiritual evolution?

Are you a Spiritual Hypochondriac seeking spiritual efficiency?

"The Answer Lies Within"

There was a time long ago, or so it seems now
Before I became who I am
When I pictured myself as a small empty cup
And yearned to be filled to the brim

I've searched for the answers so much of my life
From teachers I placed high above me
Trying on wings that simply weren't mine
In hopes that the winds would come lift me

I've pored through the books, through new and old
The rituals came and they went
The talisman's power in time left me cold
And none of it seemed heaven sent

The answer lies within my friend
The answer lies within
 The mountains can't hold it
The teachers don't own it
The answer lies within

One morning, at odds with the world I had made

I stood at my mirror in tears

But I suddenly saw that the face that stared back

Held no trace of the hunger or fears

I saw at that moment, so brilliantly clear

All the wisdom my life had collected

The student was ready, the teacher was here

In a way I have never expected

We balance our lives between ignorance and bliss

With a prayer divine wisdom will find us

And yet our greatest sin is our fear to exist

In the knowledge that God lives within us

So I don't need the mountains, the books or wings

And I don't need somebody to save me

No, all I need is to claim all the answers within

And to follow them clearly and bravely

The answer lies within, my friend

The answer lies within

-Michael B. Putman and Catherine Wilson